The Big Book of
American Facts

1000 Interesting Facts and Trivia

Bill O´Neill

ISBN-13: 978-1539068358

In this book, you'll find 1,000 funny, weird, random, and little known facts about the United States of America. From its Constitution to its molasses explosion, from its presidents' false teeth to its cow-to-resident ratios, the U.S. is full of interesting facts. Did you know that it's illegal to view a moose from an airplane in Alaska? Or that you can get a unicorn hunting license in Michigan? Now you do!

Contents

Government and Crime.. 1

Presidents 6

Food and Drink 10

History 14

Religion... 19

Geography and Nature 22

Food and Drink – Part Two 27

Language... 31

Weird Facts 34

The United States Constitution 37

Animals... 40

Laws 43

Science and Medicine 47

Big America... 50

Animals – Part Two.. 53

Planes, Trains, and Automobiles.................................. 56

Military.. 60

Laws – Part Two 64

Education 67

Sports 70

Business 74

States 78

Random Facts 81

Money...84

Inventions...87

Demographics..91

History – Part Two 95

Landmarks and Monuments 99

States – Part Two 104

Food and Drink – Part Three..................................... 108

Presidents – Part Two 112

Music 116

Random Facts – Part Two... 119

International Relations 124

Entertainment.. 129

Notable Americans 133

Big America – Part Two 137

States – Part Three... 140

Holidays 144

This book are based on random facts and written for that purpose. If you would rather read a questions and answers format, check out my other book series called <u>Trivia Madness</u>.

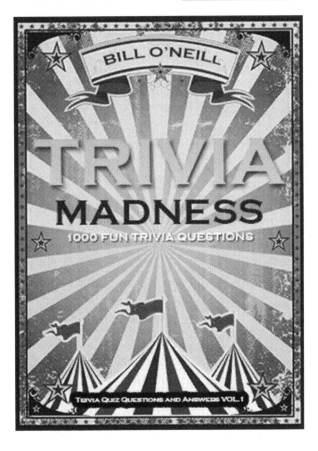

Government and Crime

1. The U.S. Library of Congress has a record of every tweet that has ever been published on Twitter.

2. About 33% of Americans have fingerprints on file with the Federal Bureau of Investigation (the FBI).

3. About 69% of American firefighters are volunteers.

4. The U.S. Supreme Court building has a basketball court on the fifth floor. Americans call it "the Highest Court in the Land."

5. American Green Cards haven't been green since 1964.

6. It is not a constitutional requirement that the U.S. Supreme Court justices have any formal legal training. James Byrnes, who was a justice from 1941 to 1942, never even attended college.

7. No one knows where the original copy of the Declaration of Independence is. There is a handwritten copy of the original in Washington, D.C.

8. Over half of all court cases in the U.S. are traffic-related.

9. A 2013 study found that the U.S. Congress was less popular among Americans than cockroaches and traffic jams.

10. The U.S. government informally determines the severity of storms by observing which Waffle House restaurants are closed due to the storm.

11. If you are running for governmental office in the U.S., doubling your spending on campaign funds will only increase your votes by 1%.

12. U.S. Supreme Court Justice Oliver Wendell was alive for so long that he was able to shake hands with both John Quincy Adams and John F. Kennedy.

13. Over 100 people born in Kentucky were elected governors of other states.

14. Fingerprinting became a standard criminal-identifying procedure in the U.S. when two Kan-

sas men with the same name were both arrested in 1903. They looked almost identical but were not related.

15. In 2015, a New York lawyer tried to settle a civil suit through trial by combat.

16. Montana's first jail was built by Henry Plummer, a notorious outlaw.

17. New York City has the lowest crime rate of all cities in North America.

18. There is a new lawsuit every 30 seconds in the United States.

19. In 2013, an exiled Romanian princess was convicted for illegally gambling and cockfighting in the state of Oregon.

20. In 1986, two women ran against each other for state governor of Nebraska. It was the first time ever that two women ran against each other for state governorship.

21. In the State House in New Hampshire, the legislature still meets in its original chambers. It's the oldest state capitol where that happens.

22. The oldest government building in the U.S. is Santa Fe, New Mexico's Palace of Governors.

23. The first professional police officer in Stewartstown, Pennsylvania was also the town lamp lighter. He was hired in 1876.

24. In California, prison inmates are used to fight forest fires.

25. The modern system of 911 emergency communications was developed in Lincoln, Nebraska.

26. In 1840, five Illinois legislators, including Abraham Lincoln, jumped out of a window to prevent a vote that could have ended the Illinois State Bank.

27. In California, Maine, Vermont, Virginia, and Washington, you don't need a law degree in order to become a lawyer.

28. In Maine and Vermont, felons are allowed to vote from prison. These are the only two states where that is permitted.

29. James Madison and Thomas Jefferson were once arrested for taking a carriage ride together in Vermont on a Sunday.

30. A Nebraska senator once tried to sue God.

31. In Independence, Missouri, there is a juvenile court that's run by juveniles. The judge and lawyers are all minors. The court's decisions are legally binding.

32. In 2000, Missouri senator Mel Carnahan was reelected to the U.S. Senate 3 weeks after his death.

33. In New Hampshire, license plates say "Live Free or Die." The plates are manufactured by state prison inmates.

34. In the 1970s, a Georgia man on death row escaped from prison the night before he was to be executed. He was killed in a bar fight later that night.

35. In the U.S., you can sue an object. The U.S. once lost a case to a sum of money.

36. The state of Colorado once had three different governors in a single day.

Presidents

1. The most common place of birth for a U.S. president is the state of Virginia.

2. If you are the president of the United States, you have the deadliest job in the country. About 1 in 10 U.S. presidents have been killed on the job.

3. U.S. President Lincoln owned a saloon.

4. Before he became president, Grover Cleveland was a sheriff in New York. He hanged a murderer as part of this job.

5. Jimmy Carter was the first U.S. president to be born in a hospital.

6. George Washington, the first president of the United States, grew hemp.

7. Barack Obama's parents met in a Russian class at the University of Hawai'i.

8. On his Inauguration Day, President Taft got stuck in his bathtub.

9. Only one U.S. president's wife was born in another country: Louisa Adams, wife of John Quincy Adams.

10. Every president of the United States who had a beard was a Republican.

11. Every president of the United States has had siblings.

12. Abraham Lincoln, the 16th president of the United States, was a licensed bartender.

13. When Thomas Jefferson and John Adams visited William Shakespeare's home in England, they broke off a piece of a chair to keep as a souvenir.

14. Princeton University's first graduate student was James Madison. Madison later became president of the United States.

15. The capital of Liberia, Monrovia, is named after U.S. president James Monroe.

16. John Quincy Adams swam naked in the Potomac River each morning when he was president of the United States.

17. U.S. President Andrew Jackson fought in dozens of duels to defend his wife's honor.

18. It is believed that U.S. President Zachary Taylor died because of some bad cherries and milk he had eaten.

19. While he was president of the United States, Franklin Pierce was arrested for running over a woman while he was riding a horse.

20. Andrew Johnson made his own suits while he was president of the United States.

21. U.S. President Ulysses S. Grant smoked at least 20 cigars every day. In 1885, he died of throat cancer.

22. U.S. President Grover Cleveland had a small tumor removed from his mouth. The tumor is currently at a museum in Philadelphia.

23. U.S. President Teddy Roosevelt was shot while giving a speech. He finished his 90-minute speech with the bullet in his chest.

24. U.S. President Herbert Hoover's son had two pet alligators. On occasion, they were allowed to walk freely through the White House.

25. U.S. President Dwight D. Eisenhower played over 800 rounds of golf while he was president.

26. U.S. President Gerald R. Ford was a fashion model when he was in college. He appeared on the cover of Cosmopolitan magazine.

27. In 1996, all three major presidential candidates were left-handed.

28. Grover Cleveland was both the 22nd and the 24th president of the United States.

Food and Drink

1. Each day in the United States, about 100 acres of pizza are sold.

2. About 22 million chickens are eaten each day in the United States.

3. The first fried dill pickle was sold in 1963 in the state of Arkansas.

4. In 1935, the cheeseburger was trademarked by Louis E. Ballast in Colorado. He owned a drive-in.

5. The lollipop was invented in 1908 in the state of Connecticut. The candy was named after a race-horse.

6. There is a town called "Popcorn" in Indiana. The state is one of the biggest corn producers in the country.

7. Most of the macadamia nuts in the world are grown on the Big Island of Hawai'i.

8. The ice cream sundae was created in Evanston, Illinois when it was illegal to sell soda on Sundays. Store owners instead sold ice cream with soda syrup and named the dish after the day of the week.

9. Maine is the U.S.'s largest producer of both lobsters and blueberries.

10. About 2 billion pounds of chocolate are consumed each year in the U.S.

11. Margarine was once illegal in Wisconsin.

12. The dry breakfast cereal industry was started when the Kellogg brothers accidentally figured out how to make flaked cereal.

13. There's only one steam-powered cider mill in the U.S. It's located in Mystic, Connecticut.

14. The world's largest strawberry shortcake was made in 1999 in Florida. It measured 827 square feet and weighed 6,000 pounds.

15. Plant City, Florida is the "Winter Strawberry Capital of the World."

16. Sumner County, Kansas is the Wheat Capital of the World.

17. Aunt Jemima pancake flour, invented in 1889 in Missouri, was the first commercial ready-mix food.

18. The Reuben sandwich was invented in Nebraska.

19. In 1719, the first potato ever planted in the U.S. was planted in New Hampshire.

20. In New Hampshire, it takes about 40 gallons of sap to make 1 gallon of maple syrup.

21. New Jersey has more diners than anywhere else in the world.

22. Over the first weekend in October, Las Cruces, New Mexico makes the world's largest enchilada.

23. Hatch, New Mexico is the Green Chile Capital of the World.

24. When the process of cellophane wrapping was invented, one effect was that the "carrot capital of the country" moved from Grants, New Mexico to California.

25. The boysenberry, a cross between several kinds of berries, was invented in the 1920s on Rudolph Boysen's farm in Northern California. Walter Knott, a Southern California berry expert and founder of the famous Knott's Berry Farm, was the first person to grow it commercially.

26. Salsa is the best selling condiment in the United States. The last condiment with that title was ketchup.

27. About 21 million hot dogs are eaten every year at baseball games in the U.S.

History

1. The first nuclear weapons were developed by the United States. They were used on Hiroshima, Japan and Nagasaki, Japan, during World War 2.

2. In 1969, American Neil Armstrong became the first man to walk on the moon.

3. About 27% of the population does not believe that a man landed on the moon in 1969.

4. During the prohibition period, the U.S. government began poisoning beer to discourage people from drinking it. This strategy resulted in thousands of deaths.

5. The current flag of the United States was designed by a high school student in 1958 for a school project. His project got a B-.

6. In the year 1620, 102 pilgrims arrived on the Mayflower. It is estimated that 10% of Americans today could be related to those 102 pilgrims.

7. Although America's Independence Day is celebrated on July 4, the country actually voted itself free from British rule on July 2, 1776.

8. America's Independence Day is celebrated on the day that John Hancock signed the Declaration of Independence. He was the first person to do so on July 4, 1776.

9. John Adams and Thomas Jefferson died on the same day in 1826: on July 4, exactly 50 years after the Declaration of Independence was signed.

10. France gave the United States its famous Statue of Liberty in 1884.

11. American Indians did not become citizens of the United States until 1924.

12. The first country to recognize the newly independent United States in 1776 was the Republic of Ragusa, which is now part of Croatia.

13. The price of corn rose 10,000% during the American Revolution because of inflation.

14. Most of the people who signed the Declaration of Independence signed it on August 2, 1776, a month after the first two signers did so.

15. The last signature on the Declaration of Independence was added 5 years after the United States declared its independence.

16. After World War II, Japan sent cherry trees to the state of Utah to symbolize friendship.

17. During the Civil War, hundreds of women dressed as men in order to serve in the war.

18. The first tourism marketing campaign for the United States was established by Captain John Smith, who began calling an area of the country "New England."

19. The world's first submarine attack occurred in 1776 in New York.

20. St. Augustine, Florida is the oldest city in the U.S. It was founded in 1565.

21. After the Declaration of Independence was signed, the signers' names were kept secret for several months to protect them. If the colonies hadn't gained independence, the signers would have been guilty of treason in England.

22. Women got the right to vote in the United States in 1920.

23. There is a crater in Iowa that was once believed to be evidence of the impact that caused the extinction of the dinosaurs. However, it was proven to be too old.

24. The first U.S. service member killed in World War II was killed by Russians.

25. Before sailing to what would eventually become the state of Virginia, John Smith fought for the Holy Roman Army, beheaded three Turks, was enslaved in Russia, and escaped by murdering his master.

26. New Hampshire declared its independence from England six months before the Declaration of Independence was signed.

27. The first women's strike in the U.S. occurred on December 30, 1828 in New Hampshire. About 400 female workers walked out of the Dover Cotton Factory, but they were forced to give in when the owners started looking for replacement workers.

28. Before World War I, pink clothing was recommended for young boys in the United States,

while blue clothing was recommended for young girls.

29. During the Depression, you could buy your movie theater tickets with canned food in Mercersburg, Pennsylvania.

30. In Taos Pueblo in New Mexico, people live in buildings that have been there for 900 years.

Religion

1. Although Protestant Christians were the majority for much of the United States' existence, only 46% of Americans identified as Protestant in 2014.

2. About 34% of Americans say they are now part of a different religion than the religion they grew up with.

3. Each week, about one in five Americans watches religious TV shows or listens to religious radio programs or Christian music.

4. When same-sex marriage was legalized in 2015 throughout the U.S., religion played a factor in how supportive Americans were. Only 24% of white evangelical Protestants in the U.S. supported gay marriage, while 82% of Americans with no religious affiliation supported it.

5. In 2014, Americans who attended religious services every week were more likely to be Republi-

cans. Americans who never went to places of worship were more likely to be Democrats.

6. In 2014, 92% of Congress identified as Christian.

7. The first Mormon Temple was built in Nauvoo, Illinois.

8. America's biggest network of charter schools is run by a Turkish imam.

9. Since 1950, only about 75 outsiders have become Amish in the United States.

10. In 1950, a church in Nebraska exploded when its choir practice was scheduled to begin. No one was injured because every single member of the choir was late to practice that day.

11. In Austin, Nevada's oldest church, the bells in the bell tower can only be rung by pulling on a rope in the men's restroom.

12. The Puritans who fled to the future United States because of religious persecution in England became known for persecuting people of other religions in the colonies.

13. The world's smallest church is located in Oneida, New York. It measures 51 by 81 inches.

14. The region with the densest Mormon population in Utah is called the "Jell-O Belt" because Mormons love Jell-O so much.

15. Connecticut once had a Bible-themed theme park called Holy Land USA.

16. The Constitution of South Carolina states that atheists cannot be governor of the state.

Geography and Nature

1. In terms of land, the United States is the fourth largest country in the world.

2. The fourth longest river system in the world is found in the United States. It consists of the Mississippi and Missouri Rivers.

3. Lake Superior has enough water to cover all of North and South America in a foot of water.

4. Three of the rivers in the United States are hundreds of millions of years old: The Susquehanna River, the New River, and the French Broad River. They are among the world's five oldest rivers.

5. When measured from its base under the sea, Mauna Kea, located in Hawai'i, is considered the tallest mountain in the world.

6. There are two separate rivers in the state of Florida that have the same name: Withlacoochee.

7. In the U.S., there are ten cities named Hollywood.

8. There are 140 towns in the U.S. that are called "Christmas" or have "Christmas" in their names.

9. In 1811, earthquakes created a 14-mile-long lake in Tennessee.

10. Badwater Basin in Death Valley, California is the lowest point in the western hemisphere. It is 282 feet below sea level.

11. The deepest lake in the U.S. is five times the height of the Statue of Liberty. It is located in the state of Oregon.

12. Almost half of the U.S. population lives in coastal regions.

13. The most common city name in the United States is "Franklin."

14. The world's largest dormant volcano, Haleakala, is located in Hawai'i.

15. 75% of U.S. land that has a higher altitude than 10,000 feet is located in Colorado.

16. There is only one place in the U.S. where four states meet: the intersection of Colorado, Arizona, New Mexico, and Utah.

17. There are only two naturally round lakes in the world. One is in DeFuniak Springs, Florida.

18. One of the world's largest single masses of exposed granite is Stone Mountain in Atlanta, Georgia.

19. There is only one natural forest in the U.S. that lies within city limits. It's in the city of Rome, Georgia.

20. The Hawaiian Islands were formed by underwater volcanoes that erupted thousands of years ago.

21. The world's most active volcano is Kilauea, located in Hawai'i.

22. In Kentucky, there's a cave that contains the shortest and deepest underground river in the world.

23. The islands of Nantucket and Martha's Vineyard in Massachusetts were formed by glaciers during the ice age.

24. No matter where you stand in the state of Michigan, you will always be within 85 miles of a Great Lake.

25. In 2014, the Colorado River reached the ocean for the first time in 16 years.

26. The Kilauea Volcano in Hawai'i has been erupting continuously for 30 years.

27. The state of South Dakota is home to the largest natural warm water pool in the world.

28. The world's 2 shortest rivers are in Oregon and Montana. Their lengths are between 58 feet and 200 feet.

29. There is only one city in the U.S. built inside of a meteor crater. It's Middlesboro, Kentucky.

30. The world's largest indoor rain forest is the Lied Jungle in Omaha, Nebraska.

31. The exact midpoint between Boston and San Francisco is Kearney, Nebraska.

32. If you want to drive from Los Angeles, California to Reno, Nevada, you'll be driving west.

33. The New River is the oldest river in the United
States.

Food and Drink – Part Two

1. Marshmallows and Jell-O were invented in the same New York city of Rochester.

2. Apples were introduced to New York in the 1600s by European settlers.

3. North Carolina's official state drink is milk.

4. In 1982, according to the Guinness Book of World Records, Rutland, North Dakota cooked the world's largest hamburger. It weighed 3591 pounds.

5. The first hot dog was served in Ohio in the year 1900.

6. There is only one state that has an official state nut. It's Oregon, and the official nut is the hazelnut.

7. Kennett Square, Pennsylvania is the mushroom capital of the world.

8. In 1927, the powdered drink Kool-Aid was invented in Nebraska.

9. The official state question of New Mexico is "Red or green?" It refers to restaurants asking customers if they'd prefer red or green chilies in their food.

10. In Vermont, the ice cream company Ben and Jerry's has an actual graveyard for retired ice cream flavors.

11. A Vermont brewery once created a garlic flavored beer. It was quickly labeled "undrinkable."

12. Nebraska's official state drink is Kool-Aid.

13. There is a cave in Missouri filled with $4 billion worth of milk fat for cheese and butter.

14. Sliced bread was banned in the U.S. for a short while in 1943.

15. About 350 slices of pizza are eaten every second in the United States.

16. In Iowa, a "Snickers salad" is chopped up Snickers candy, green apples, and whipped topping.

17. A whiskey can only qualify as a bourbon if it was made in the United States.

18. There is a mayonnaise store in New York City that only sells mayonnaise. It makes 12 flavors.

19. Fortune cookies were invented in the United States, not China.

20. In the United States, Kinder Eggs are illegal.

21. Most American chicken meat is split in half and sent around the world. White chicken meat is sold in the U.S., while the chicken's dark meat is sold in Russia and Asia due to local preferences.

22. The hottest pepper in the world is the South Carolina-grown Carolina Reaper, which can be twice as hot as the ghost pepper.

23. Clark, South Dakota hosts a Mashed Potato Wrestling Contest.

24. The world's only Corn Palace is located in Mitchell, South Dakota.

25. On Super Bowl Sunday each year, Americans eat about 1.25 billion chicken wings.

26. The U.S. grows over 200 varieties of watermelon.

27. Over 17 million gallons of wine are produced in California every year.

28. The first ever soft serve ice cream machine debuted at a Dairy Queen location in the state of Washington.

29. Wisconsin is home to the world's largest mustard collection. It's housed in a museum that celebrates an annual National Mustard Day.

Language

1. Spanish is the second-most spoken language in the United States. English is the first.

2. The United States has no official national language.

3. The word "dude" was coined in the state of Wyoming at the Eaton Dude Ranch.

4. There are more Spanish speakers in the United States than in Spain.

5. The Hawaiian alphabet has only 12 letters. Almost half are vowels.

6. The only letter in the English alphabet that isn't in any U.S. state name is Q.

7. The Arkansas River is pronounced "ar-KAN-zus" in Kansas, but it's pronounced "AR-kan-saw" in Colorado and Oklahoma.

8. In the U.S., there are more Tagalog speakers than Vietnamese, Korean, German, Arabic, or Russian speakers.

9. According to the State Constitution of New Mexico, the state is officially bilingual. A third of New Mexican families speak Spanish in the home.

10. In New Mexico, there are descendants of Spanish conquistadors who speak a variety of 16th century Spanish that's no longer spoken anywhere else in the world.

11. U.S. President Martin van Buren spoke Dutch as a first language. English was his second language.

12. In 1885, the first daily Yiddish newspaper was established in New York City.

13. Between 1923 and 1969, "American" was the official language of the state of Illinois.

14. In 1919, Nebraska tried to make foreign language instruction illegal.

15. Including people who speak Spanish as a second language, the U.S. is the second largest Spanish-speaking country in the world.

16. Before World War I, German was the second most spoken language in the U.S. It was suppressed during the war.

17. The third most used language in the United States, after English and Spanish, is American Sign Language.

Weird Facts

1. In 1919, 2 million gallons of molasses exploded out of a tank in Boston. It killed 21 people.

2. In 1922 at the Los Angeles County fair, one attraction demonstrated how to make toothpaste out of oranges.

3. In 1945, a farmer cut off a chicken's head in Colorado. The chicken stayed alive and lived for 4 years without a head.

4. In 1820 in New Jersey, tomatoes were put on trial at a courthouse to prove they weren't poisonous.

5. In 1972, a man stole $500,000 on an airplane and accidentally dropped the money over a farm in Indiana while he was parachuting out of the plane.

6. The state of Arkansas hosts an annual World's Championship Duck Calling Contest.

7. In colonial New England, pumpkins were used as tools for haircuts. It was in fashion to cut hair in a round uniform style, so pumpkins were perfect guides for these "pumpkin head" New Englanders.

8. Pelicans will rip off their own flesh to feed their young rather than let them starve. Because of this, the first governor of Louisiana used pelican symbols on official documents.

9. The total weight of all earthworms in the U.S. is 55 times heavier than the total weight of all Americans.

10. Some of Gandhi's ashes are now in Southern California.

11. Stonewall Jackson's arm has a grave in a Virginia cemetery.

12. In the 1920s in New York City, there was a tradition of knocking straw hats off of men's heads if they were wearing a straw hat after September 15.

13. There is a spoon museum in New Jersey. It contains over 5,400 spoons from around the world.

14. There was once a resident of Mississippi who often snuck into people's homes and cut their hair while they were asleep.

15. There is a university in Michigan that offers unicorn hunting licenses.

16. In Taos, New Mexico, there is a constant humming sound that only 2% of the population can hear. No one knows what the sound is from.

The United States Constitution

1. The word "Pennsylvania" is misspelled as "Pensylvania" in the Constitution.

2. The original draft of the U.S. Constitution is both the oldest and the shortest government constitution in the world.

3. The oldest person to sign the Constitution of the United States was Ben Franklin. He was 81 years old.

4. The youngest person to sign the Constitution was 26 years old. His name was Jonathan Dayton.

5. Only 2 presidents signed the Constitution: George Washington and James Madison.

6. The holiday of Thanksgiving was originally intended to celebrate the new Constitution of the United States.

7. The men who wrote the Constitution of the United States believed that pure democracy was dangerous. They founded the country as a republic instead.

8. The Bill of Rights, now considered an important part of the Constitution of the United States, was not ratified until 15 years after the Constitution was written.

9. It took 100 days to write the United States Constitution.

10. The writers of the Constitution of the United States worked on the document with the windows closed all summer in order to ensure secrecy.

11. When it was first written, the Constitution of the United States was largely unpopular among people living in the States.

12. Rhode Island was the last state to approve of the Constitution. It did so in May of 1790.

13. Delaware was the first state to approve of the Constitution of the United States.

14. In 1919, the United States amended its constitution to make alcohol illegal. In 1933, it amended its constitution again to legalize alcohol.

15. Thomas Jefferson proposed that the U.S. Constitution expire every 19 years.

16. The 27th amendment to the U.S. Constitution was ratified over 200 years after the first state approved it. It restricts the power of Congress to raise its own pay.

Animals

1. 98% of the world's crayfish are located in the state of Louisiana.

2. The state of Florida is the only place in the world where there are both alligators and crocodiles.

3. Benjamin Franklin nominated the turkey as the emblem of the United States. It lost to the bald eagle.

4. Catalina Island in California is home to a significant buffalo population. The buffalo were first brought to the island in 1924 as part of a film set and were simply left behind when the filming had finished.

5. A successful goldfish farm was founded in 1899 in the state of Indiana.

6. In 1874, the Lincoln Park Zoo in Chicago, Illinois bought its first animal. It was a bear cub, purchased for $10.

7. Rayne, Louisiana is the Frog Capital of the World.

8. Gueydan, Louisiana is the Duck Capital of America.

9. Michigan is known as the Wolverine State. However, there are no wolverines in Michigan anymore.

10. Washington, D.C. has an official dinosaur. Its fossil was discovered in the city in 1898.

11. In South Dakota's Fountain Inn, horses are only allowed inside if they are wearing pants.

12. The biggest migratory elk herd in the U.S. is located in Montana.

13. There can be up to 1,700 nesting pelicans at the Bowdoin National Wildlife Refuge in Montana.

14. Dinosaur eggs were discovered at Egg Mountain in Montana.

15. Montana has more mammal species than any other state.

16. There are over 8,000 moose in Montana. In the 1900s, it was thought that they were extinct in the area.

17. Montana's elk, deer, and antelope populations are larger than Montana's human population.

18. In Georgia, it's illegal to keep a donkey in a bathtub.

19. Venice, Florida is the Shark Tooth Capital of the World.

20. The "Teddy Bear" was inspired by President Theodore Roosevelt, who was depicted in a cartoon as sparing a bear while hunting.

21. California's official state animal is the grizzly bear. However, no one has seen a grizzly bear in California since 1922.

22. The world's largest woolly mammoth fossil was found in Nebraska.

Laws

1. In the U.S., it's legal for children to smoke cigarettes. However, it is illegal for anyone under the age of 18 to purchase them.

2. In the state of Florida, it's illegal to sing in public while wearing a swimsuit.

3. In the state of Idaho, it's illegal to fish while on the back of a camel.

4. In the state of Kentucky, it's illegal to hold ice cream in your back pocket.

5. Hunting camels is illegal in the state of Arizona.

6. The legal drinking age in the U.S. is 21. It is the highest in the world.

7. It's illegal for chickens to cross the street in Quitman, Georgia.

8. Cigarette ads were banned from U.S. television in 1971.

9. In Pacific Grove, California, it's illegal to molest monarch butterflies.

10. On the Hawaiian island of Kauai, it is illegal to build a building that is taller than a palm tree.

11. U.S. cattle branding began when Connecticut farmers were legally required to mark each of their pigs.

12. Gainesville, Georgia is the Chicken Capital of the World. However, it's illegal to eat chicken with a fork there.

13. In Idaho, it's illegal to give someone a box of candy that weighs over 50 pounds.

14. It was once illegal to sell ice cream sodas on Sundays in Evanston, Illinois.

15. It's illegal for boys to throw snowballs at trees in Mount Pulaski, Illinois. It's perfectly legal for girls to do so.

16. Billboards are illegal in Hawai'i, Alaska, Maine, and Vermont.

17. It's illegal to cross the street walking on your hands in Hartford, Connecticut.

18. Kansas once had a law that made it illegal to serve cherry pie with ice cream on top.

19. In Louisiana, it's legally considered more aggressive to bite someone with false teeth rather than natural teeth.

20. In Alabama, it's illegal to wear a mask in public.

21. Bear wrestling is illegal in the state of Alabama.

22. In Lee County, Alabama, it's illegal to sell peanuts on Wednesday nights.

23. If you put salt on a railroad track in Alabama, you may face the death penalty.

24. In Alaska, it's illegal to view moose from airplanes.

25. It's illegal to be drunk in a mine in Wyoming.

26. In Wyoming, women are not legally allowed to drink while standing within 5 feet of a bar.

27. It's illegal to whistle underwater in West Virginia.

28. In West Virginia, it was once illegal to own a red or black flag.

29. In Wisconsin, it's illegal to serve apple pie without cheese in restaurants.

30. Tattooing is illegal in Brookfield, Wisconsin. However, it's legal if it's done for medical purposes.

31. Between 1838 and 1976, it was legal to kill Mormons in Missouri.

32. Firing missiles in South Carolina is legal as long as you have a permit.

Science and Medicine

1. For research purposes for the Manhattan Project, 18 people were injected with plutonium to test how nuclear weapons would affect humans.

2. At a hospital in Las Vegas in 1980, workers were suspended because they were betting on when patients would die.

3. Lyme disease got its name from Lyme, Connecticut, where several people had the disease in 1975.

4. The third leading cause of death in the United States is medical mistakes made in hospitals.

5. The world's first human lung transplant was conducted in 1963 at the University of Mississippi Medical Center.

6. The first heart transplant surgery in the world was completed in 1964 in Mississippi.

7. Between the 1950s and 1970s, U.S. pediatrician Saul Krugman infected thousands of mentally

disabled children with Hepatitis for research purposes.

8. When flights were grounded on 9/11, one plane was allowed to fly from San Diego to Florida. It was carrying anti-venom to save the life of a snake keeper who had been bitten. The only other usable anti-venom was in New York.

9. In 1885, Dr. George Holtzapple discovered how to use oxygen to help patients. He did so in response to a 16-year-old patient in Pennsylvania who was about to die of pneumonia.

10. The largest chemical producing state in the U.S. is New Jersey.

11. The atomic bomb museum in New Mexico is only open for 12 hours per year.

12. In 1941, the world's highest quality penicillin was found in a moldy cantaloupe in Illinois.

13. Ten-thousand-year-old arrowheads were found on the same New Mexican ground where modern missiles are tested.

14. Due to radiation from the sun, all of the American flags on the Moon are now white.

15. In 2006, a 12-year-old's science project discovered that most ice in Florida fast food restaurants was dirtier than toilet water.

16. In 1976, a chemistry student in Maryland accidentally gave himself Parkinson's disease while trying to make opioids. His mistake advanced Parkinson's research.

17. In Texas, you need a permit to buy glassware for chemistry.

18. A California biology professor brewed beer from yeast found in a 45-million-year-old insect.

Big America

1. The United States has the third largest population in the world, after China and India.

2. The Midwest of the United States is home to most of the world's tornadoes.

3. More petroleum is consumed in the United States than in any other country in the world.

4. 33% of the U.S. population is considered obese.

5. The city of Tucson, Arizona has more telescopes than anywhere else in the world.

6. There are more bagpipes in the U.S. than in Scotland.

7. One-fourth of the world's energy is consumed in the United States.

8. The world's largest man-made waterfall is in Redding, California.

9. Berry College in the state of Georgia is the world's largest college campus.

10. Mountain View, Arkansas is one of the largest dulcimer producers in the world.

11. The world's largest landlocked harbor is thought to be San Francisco Bay.

12. The world's largest poultry convention, the International Poultry Trade Show, is hosted in the state of Georgia each year.

13. The city of Honolulu, Hawai'i has the longest borders of any city in the world.

14. The world's biggest telescope is located in Hawai'i.

15. The world's largest manufacturer of magic supplies is in Colon, Michigan.

16. 25 adults can sit on the largest porch swing in the world. It's located in Hebron, Nebraska.

17. The largest hand-planted forest in the world is in Nebraska.

18. Las Vegas, Nevada has more hotel rooms than anywhere else in the world.

19. The world's tallest water tower is located in New Jersey.

20. The amount of land used in the U.S. to cultivate corn is as big as all of Germany.

21. The largest helium well in the world is located in Amarillo, Texas.

22. The world's largest nugget of silver was found in the state of Colorado.

23. The world's longest boardwalk is located in Atlantic City, New Jersey.

24. Outside of the Middle East, the largest petroleum containment area is in New Jersey.

25. The largest sycamore tree in the world is in the state of West Virginia.

Animals – Part Two

1. In Sparks, Nevada, an elephant named Bertha performed at a casino for 37 years.

2. The kangaroo rat, which lives in Death Valley, Nevada, can live its entire life without drinking any liquid.

3. As late as 1870, camels were used as pack animals in Nevada.

4. New Mexico's state animal is the black bear in honor of Smokey the Bear. Smokey was found trapped in a tree in 1950 when the forest he lived in was destroyed in a fire.

5. New Mexico has more sheep and cattle than people.

6. There are annual duck races in Deming, New Mexico.

7. In 2015, a 22-year-old burglar was killed by an alligator. He was one of 3 people killed by alligators that year in the United States.

8. The state of Florida once named a hippo an honorary citizen.

9. The largest state-owned sheep research center in the U.S. is housed at North Dakota State University.

10. North Dakota is home to the world's largest buffalo monument. It weighs 60 tons.

11. The first public zoo in the U.S. was founded by Benjamin Franklin.

12. South Carolina has an official state amphibian: the salamander.

13. There is a jaguar population living in Arizona and New Mexico. The animal is native to North America.

14. The U.S. is home to the largest population of tigers in the world. There are more tigers in captivity than there are in the wild.

15. In 1986, a small town in Texas elected a goat as its mayor. The goat enjoyed drinking beer.

16. In the United States, you're more likely to be killed by a cow than by a shark.

17. Honeybees were introduced to North America by the early European settlers. The bees are not native to the U.S.

18. There are more bat species in Texas than in any other part of the U.S.

19. North Dakota is known for its flickertails, squirrels that flick or jerk their tails while running.

20. Vermont has the largest ratio of dairy cows to people in the U.S.

21. The United States is home to 47 different sheep breeds.

Planes, Trains, and Automobiles

1. There are about 845 cars for every 1,000 people in the United States.

2. The helicopter was invented in Connecticut in 1939.

3. The first-ever U.S. automobile law was passed in 1901 in Connecticut. It set the speed limit at 12 miles per hour.

4. Connecticut was the first state to make permanent license plates for cars. It began doing so in 1937.

5. The first recorded automobile accident happened in 1896. A New York City driver hit a bicyclist and spent a night in jail.

6. The first mass-produced automobile in the U.S. was produced in Detroit in 1901. An assembly line was used to make 425 cars.

7. Between 1942 and 1945, every American automobile manufacturer was required to make military vehicles. It was illegal to manufacture civilian or commercial automobiles during the war.

8. The U.S. auto industry employed the most people in the year 2000. That year, 1.3 million people worked in the industry.

9. In the mid-20th century, General Motors, Ford, and Chrysler were producing two-thirds of all cars sold around the world.

10. At the Boston University Bridge in Boston, a boat can sail under a train moving under a car driving under an airplane. It's the only place in the world where that can happen.

11. The world has only one open railroad bridge made of both cast iron and wrought iron. It's located in Savage, Maryland.

12. The U.S. government paid 22 million dollars to build the largest airplane that had ever been built in 1947. The plane's flight lasted for one minute. It never flew again.

13. The U.S.'s first subway system was built in Boston.

14. Northwest Airlines, based in Minnesota, was the first major airline to prohibit smoking on international flights.

15. The car theft capital of the world is Newark, New Jersey. There are more cars stolen there than in New York City and Los Angeles combined.

16. The largest ship used by Christopher Columbus on his voyage to the Americas was only slightly larger than a modern coach bus.

17. There are 722 miles of subway tracks in New York City.

18. The first railroad in the U.S. was 11 miles long. It was located in New York.

19. The first state to require cars to have license plates was New York.

20. The first traffic light in the United States was installed in Cleveland, Ohio in 1914.

21. The first city to use police cars was Akron, Ohio.

22. Until 1977, the U.S. had a presidential yacht.

23. Car company Subaru first advertised its cars in the United States as "cheap and ugly."

24. Delaware is the only state that you can't fly to on a commercial flight.

Military

1. The United States has the largest air force in the world.

2. In 1775, the U.S. navy had a total of 4 ships.

3. Only about 25% of Americans between the ages of 17 and 23 years old are qualified to serve in the military.

4. Mapping North America was once a duty of the U.S. Army.

5. U.S. military facilities occupy an area that is larger than all of Washington, D.C., Massachusetts, and New Jersey put together.

6. The U.S. Coast Guard confiscates about 306 pounds of cocaine every day.

7. In 2008, the United States spent more money in Iraq every 5 seconds than the amount of money an average American earned in the whole year.

8. If all of the retired U.S. memorial ships formed a navy, it would be the third largest in the world.

9. In the U.S. military, commanders can punish their troops by restricting their diet to only bread and water--but only while aboard a ship.

10. In 2001, the U.S. military sent troops on horse-back into Afghanistan.

11. There is a stuffed one-legged pigeon on display at the National Museum of the U.S. Air Force. The pigeon is considered a World War I war hero.

12. The sailing capital of the world is Annapolis, Maryland. It is also where the United States Naval Academy is located.

13. In 1941, a U.S. sailor was dishonorably dis-charged when he took down a Nazi flag in San Francisco. He was reinstated when the war be-gan.

14. M&M's, heat-resistant and easily transportable chocolate candies, were originally created for U.S. soldiers serving in World War II.

15. The first emergency chocolate ration given to U.S. Army soldiers was supposed to taste "only a

bit better than a boiled potato" so that soldiers would only eat the chocolate in real emergency situations.

16. During World War II, the Korean War, and the Vietnam War, women volunteered with the American Red Cross to serve donuts to American soldiers in theaters of war.

17. Hitler's nephew served in the U.S. Navy.

18. A rocket testing missile range was built on the same land in New Mexico where the world's first atomic bomb was detonated.

19. The United States has 19 aircraft carriers. The rest of the world combined also has 19.

20. During the War of 1812, New York meatpacker Sam Wilson stamped "U.S. Beef" on his products. Soldiers interpreted the "U.S." as standing for "Uncle Sam."

21. Members of the New York Guard, the state militia, don't have to pay tolls in the state. Basic training lasts one week.

22. In 1861, the entire student body at the University of Mississippi joined the Confederate Army. Eve-

ry one of them was killed, captured, or wounded in the Civil War.

23. In 1961, the U.S. military accidentally dropped two nuclear bombs over North Carolina.

24. Only one person in U.S. history was both an admiral in the Navy and a general in the Army. His name was Samuel Powhatan Carter, and he was born in Elizabethton, Tennessee.

Laws – Part Two

1. In Texas, it's legal for parents to serve their underage children alcohol. However, parents may be prosecuted if the child gets hurt.

2. In South Dakota, it's illegal to fall asleep in a cheese factory.

3. In the state of South Dakota, it's legal to shoot Native Americans if there are more than 5 on your property.

4. Rhode Island has a law stating that it's illegal to bite off another person's leg.

5. In Providence, Rhode Island, it's illegal to sell both toothpaste and a toothbrush to the same customer on a Sunday.

6. Selling your eye is illegal in Texas.

7. Milking another person's cow is illegal in Texas.

8. In Iowa, it's illegal for men with moustaches to kiss women in public.

9. In Blue Hill, Nebraska, it's illegal for a woman wearing a hat that would scare a timid person to be seen eating onions in public.

10. On New Mexico's Indian Reservations, tribal law can supersede state law.

11. In Hazelton, Pennsylvania, it's illegal to drink a carbonated beverage while lecturing in a school auditorium.

12. The state of New Mexico passed a law affirming that Pluto is, in fact, a planet.

13. In Pennsylvania, it's illegal to use milk crates for anything other than milk.

14. It's illegal to be an elephant in Vermont.

15. The only state where it's legal to drive while drinking an alcoholic beverage is Mississippi.

16. In Kennesaw, Georgia, all families are legally required to own a gun.

17. In 1969, men could only drink at bars in Atlanta, Georgia if they were wearing suits and ties.

18. Youth cage fighting is legal in Missouri.

19. Idaho is the only state that has a law specifically outlawing cannibalism.

20. It's illegal to sell alcohol on Thanksgiving in North Dakota and Massachusetts.

21. In West Virginia, there is a town where phones and wifi are illegal due to the presence of a government telescope.

22. In South Carolina, if you hit a deer with your car, you can receive a tax credit if you donate the meat to charity.

23. In 1973, pay toilets were banned in the U.S. Arguing that the toilets were discriminatory against women, feminists played a major role in their prohibition.

Education

1. The oldest public library in the U.S. opened in 1771 in Connecticut. Patrons were fined for "greasing," or the wax that dripped onto books while reading by candlelight.

2. The world's first college that was chartered to grant degrees to women was Wesleyan College in Macon, Georgia.

3. There are more malls than high schools in the United States.

4. In 1908, the New York Board of Education prohibited whipping children in schools.

5. At Brigham Young University, you need a doctor's note to grow a beard.

6. The first school in the U.S. opened in 1696 in Maryland.

7. At the University of California, Berkeley, 16 elements on the periodic table were discovered.

8. Thomas Jefferson designed several buildings on the University of Virginia campus.

9. Hawai'i's Big Island has more scientific observatories than anywhere else in the world.

10. Americans spend more money on shoes and jewelry than they do on higher education.

11. In 1858, a nearly complete dinosaur skeleton was discovered in New Jersey. The discovery launched modern paleontology, the study of dinosaur fossils.

12. The state of New Mexico had no public colleges or high schools until 1888.

13. Only about half of U.S. college students complete their degrees.

14. There is only one school in the world that offers a Bachelor of Science degree with a Cosmetics and Fragrance Marketing major. It's the Fashion Institute of Technology in New York.

15. In 1893, New Mexico State University had a total of one graduating student. He was murdered before graduation.

16. The state of Indiana tried to pass a law making Pi equal to 3.2.

17. In Freeport, Illinois, there is a high school whose mascot is a pretzel.

18. Utah is the only state that has more men than women in college.

19. 17 of the world's 20 top ranking universities are in the United States.

20. In the U.S., the official academic color for Accountancy is "Drab."

21. The U.S. Pledge of Allegiance, which is commonly recited in American public schools, was created by a magazine trying to sell American flags to schools.

22. The first woman to earn a PhD in Computer Science in the U.S. was a Catholic nun.

23. In all schools in San Diego, California, hypnotism is banned.

Sports

1. In 2010, the number of Americans that played basketball was almost double the number of Americans that played baseball.

2. The sport with the highest number of female players in the United States is volleyball.

3. In 2010, American football teams spent $358 million on uniforms.

4. The only U.S. state in history to decide not to host the Olympics when offered was Colorado. In 1976, Colorado voters decided not to host the Winter Olympics.

5. The only athlete to ever win 7 gold medals in the Olympics in a single year was a swimmer who attended Indiana University.

6. The sport of volleyball was created in Massachusetts in 1895. It was originally called "mintonette."

7. Springfield, Massachusetts was home to the first basketball game. It was played in 1891.

8. Stickball is America's oldest game. It was played by the Choctaw Indians of Mississippi.

9. Samoan Americans are 50 times more likely to play in the NFL, the U.S. National Football League, than Americans who are not ethnically Samoan.

10. At one football game in the 1980s, Louisiana State University fans were so loud after a touchdown that their celebration registered as an earthquake.

11. In 1871, the first professional baseball game was played in Fort Wayne, Indiana.

12. Worcester, Massachusetts once had a Major League Baseball team named the Worcester Worcesters.

13. The first person to be photographed giving the middle finger was Charles Radbourn, a Major League Baseball pitcher in Boston. The photo was taken in 1886.

14. Frisbees were invented in 1871 when students in Connecticut began tossing Frisbie Pie plates as a game.

15. Ice polo and hockey are the only sports that don't need licenses to play professional games on Sundays in Rhode Island.

16. In 1905, a Chicago Cubs baseball fan caught and kept a fly ball while sitting in the bleachers. The president of the baseball team then filed charges against him.

17. Alaska's official state sport is dog mushing.

18. The first baseball game was played in Hoboken, New Jersey.

19. The first intercollegiate football game in the U.S. occurred in New Brunswick, New Jersey in 1869. It was Rutgers College against Princeton, and Rutgers won.

20. The longest game in baseball history lasted for 33 innings. Rochester was playing the Pawtucket Red Sox in New York.

21. Fayetteville, North Carolina was the site of the first miniature golf course.

22. In 1924, the U.S. won the last ever Olympic gold medal for rugby. Technically, that makes them still reigning champions.

23. All of Pittsburgh's sports teams share the same colors: black and gold.

24. The world's first international cricket match was held between the United States and Canada in 1844. Canada won.

25. In the 1904 Olympic games, the United States won the gold, silver, and bronze medals for Tug of War.

26. 14 of the 25 biggest sports stadiums in the world belong to American college football teams.

27. American baseball player Babe Ruth kept a wet cabbage leaf under his cap during games to stay cool.

Business

1. 1 out of every 8 Americans has worked at McDonald's at some point in their lives.

2. Apple, the company that created the iPhone, is worth more money than the U.S. Treasury.

3. The average American spends 4 and a half years at a single job.

4. In most U.S. states, a football coach is the highest paid public employee.

5. It is estimated that almost half of America's jobs could soon be lost to robots and computers.

6. Walmart is the largest employer in 21 states in the U.S.

7. The state of Maryland has more millionaires per capita than any other U.S. state.

8. 1% of Americans own more wealth than the bottom 50% of Americans combined.

9. In 1993, the government of the United States spent $277,000 on pickle research.

10. The largest employer in the United States is the Department of Defense.

11. Coca-Cola was invented in Atlanta, Georgia in 1886 by Dr. John Pemberton. Pemberton's bookkeeper wrote "Coca-Cola" as it still appears all around the world today.

12. One of America's first female millionaires made her money from a hair straightening treatment.

13. Pizza Hut first opened in Wichita, Kansas.

14. The first McDonald's opened in Des Plaines, Illinois.

15. There is one McDonald's in the world that has turquoise arches. It's located in Sedona, Arizona.

16. On June 17, 1994, Domino's Pizza hit record sales. On that day, over 95 million people were watching the pursuit of O.J. Simpson on TV.

17. Post-It Notes are made exclusively in Cynthiana, Kentucky. It's a secret how many notes are made per year.

18. The Teletubbies were brought to the U.S. by Meg Whitman, former CEO of Ebay.

19. In North Jersey, there are seven major shopping malls within 25 square miles. That's the most shopping malls in one area in the whole world.

20. In 1997, the owner of a glass replacement company in Brooklyn, New York was arrested because he started breaking windows to increase business.

21. There are five times as many storage facilities as there are Starbucks locations in the United States.

22. The oldest running tavern in the U.S., the White Horse Tavern, is located in Rhode Island. It was established in 1673.

23. Burger King stole its name from a restaurant in Matoon, Illinois.

24. In Colorado, there are three times as many marijuana dispensaries as Starbucks locations.

25. The absolute farthest you can get from a McDonald's in the 48 contiguous states is 107 miles.

26. According to the Guinness Book of World Records, the quietest place in the world is at Microsoft in Redmond, Washington.

27. For a short period, Apple was wealthier than the United States.

28. There is only one U.S. state capital that doesn't have a McDonalds. It's Montpelier, Vermont.

29. Vermont was the only state without a Wal-Mart until 1996.

30. Ben & Jerry's Ice Cream gives their ice cream waste products to local Vermont farmers to feed their hogs.

31. The United States has 46,990 shopping malls.

32. Roswell, New Mexico was founded when a professional gambler established a single store on a cattle trail.

States

1. Alaska, the largest U.S. state, was purchased from Russia in 1867.

2. Hawai'i, the last state to become part of the United States, is made up entirely of islands.

3. In the state of Montana, there are 3 times more cows than people.

4. The state of Rhode Island is 429 times smaller than Alaska. However, Rhode Island has a larger population than Alaska.

5. The state of Alaska touches more ocean water than all of the other U.S. states combined.

6. The city of Juneau, Alaska is bigger than the whole state of Delaware.

7. Hawai'i is the only U.S. state that grows coffee commercially.

8. "Hell" is a real town in the state of Michigan.

9. There is a higher percentage of people who walk to work in Alaska than in any other state.

10. Wyoming was the first state to allow women to vote.

11. The license plates in the state of Wyoming have bucking broncos on them.

12. The state of Wyoming produces 3 million tons of coal each week.

13. The least populated state in the U.S. is Wyoming.

14. The official song of the state of Alabama is called "Alabama."

15. There is a county in Alabama that is older than the state.

16. The state of California has more shopping malls than any other state.

17. The state flag of Alaska was designed by a 13-year0old in 1926.

18. A third of Alaska is in the Arctic Circle.

19. The official state drink of Arkansas is milk.

20. Santa Fe, New Mexico was founded in 1610. It is the oldest state capital in the United States.

21. The state of Alaska is 425 times the size of the state of Rhode Island.

22. There is only one state with no national parks, seashores, monuments, historic sites, or memorials recognized by the National Park System. That state is Delaware.

23. The state of Hawai'i has its own time zone (Hawaiian Standard Time).

24. There is only one state that doesn't have counties: Louisiana. It has parishes instead.

25. The state of Louisiana refers to Napoleonic Code in its state law.

26. There is only one state in the U.S. whose name has just one syllable: Maine.

27. The only state name that can be typed on a single row of keys is Alaska.

28. In the state of Delaware, there are 50,000 more corporations than people.

Random Facts

1. There are 13,092 forks, knives, and spoons in the White House.

2. In the city of Atlanta, there are more than 50 streets called "Peachtree."

3. In Colorado, a road mile marker that read "420" kept getting stolen. State officials replaced the sign with one that read "419.99" instead.

4. The Pentagon building in Arlington, Virginia has about 68,000 miles of internal telephone lines.

5. The official names of the colors on the United States flag are "White," "Old Glory Red," and "Old Glory Blue."

6. The only currently active U.S. diamond mine is located in the state of Arkansas.

7. The most popular street name in the United States is "Second Street."

8. Over 10% of the salt in the world is used to melt ice on American roads.

9. One of the first two navel orange trees brought to the U.S. in 1875 is still alive today.

10. The famous pirate Blackbeard was killed in North Carolina in 1718.

11. The state of Alabama has a museum that houses Hitler's typewriter.

12. Alpine County, California has no banks, ATMs, dentists, traffic lights, or high schools. There are seven counties in California that are even smaller than Alpine.

13. You can drive a car through the post office on West Van Buren Street in Chicago, Illinois.

14. The Garden of Eden in Lucas, Kansas was made with over 100 tons of concrete.

15. Barren County has the most fertile land in the state of Kentucky.

16. 90% of toothpicks made in the U.S. are made in the state of Maine.

17. Scottsboro, Alabama has an "Unclaimed Baggage Center." The facility purchases lost luggage from airlines.

18. There is one all-water mail route in the U.S. It's in the city of Magnolia Springs, Alabama, where all mail is delivered by boat.

19. The first successful manned balloon launch in the U.S. was completed by a 13-year-old in 1784.

20. There is a decoy capital of the world. It's Havre de Grace, Maryland.

21. Michigan has a floating post office--the only one in the world. It delivers mail to ships at sea.

Money

1. It costs almost 2 cents to make a penny (worth 1 cent). It costs around 9 cents to make a single nickel (worth 5 cents).

2. 47% of Americans put no money into savings accounts.

3. Between 1942 and 1945, nickels (coins worth 5 U.S. cents) were made with no nickel in them.

4. In 1825, it wasn't possible to visit the Philadelphia Mint when it was raining.

5. The Capitol building in Arizona has enough copper on the roof to make 4,800,000 pennies.

6. There is an ATM in Miami designed specifically for rollerbladers.

7. The one-dollar bill contains a hidden image of a spider in the upper corner.

8. In Fort Knox, Kentucky, there is over $6 billion worth of gold stored in underground vaults. It's the largest amount of gold stored in the whole world.

9. In 1915, a three-minute telephone call from New York to San Francisco cost $20.70.

10. In 1888, there were more millionaires per capita in Helena, Montana than in any other city in the world.

11. Fairfield County, Connecticut has a higher wealth disparity than Saudi Arabia, Qatar, and the UAE.

12. The first self-made female millionaire in the United States was black.

13. The currency of colonial Vermont was the nil-lyweiner. The treasury secretary was named Pimpy McGrundel.

14. The last time that the U.S. had no national debt was January 8, 1836.

15. The first official U.S. cent was designed by Benjamin Franklin. It contained the words "mind your business."

16. 65% of all $100 bills made in the U.S. end up in foreign countries.

17. U.S. dollar bills, often called "paper money," are 75% cotton.

18. The U.S. $5 bill only lasts for about 16 months in circulation.

Inventions

1. The first city in the world to be lit by electricity was Wabash, Indiana.

2. In 1933, the first drive-in movie theater in the world opened in New Jersey.

3. The typewriter was invented in 1867 in the state of Wisconsin.

4. The world's first nuclear submarine was built in 1954 in Groton, Connecticut.

5. The first Polaroid camera was invented in Connecticut in 1934.

6. Color television first debuted in Connecticut in 1948.

7. In 1836, the town of Simsbury, Connecticut began to manufacture the first safety fuse.

8. In 1944, the first sunscreen was invented in Miami by a man who cooked cocoa butter in a coffee pot on his kitchen stove.

9. Thomas Edison showed an electric light to the public for the first time at the Southern Exposition in Kentucky in 1883.

10. The first skyscraper building in the world was erected in Chicago in 1885.

11. The first nuclear fission reactor was built in a squash court at the University of Chicago.

12. The machine gun was invented in 1862 in Indiana.

13. In 1892, a man in Kentucky invented the radio.

14. The drinking straw was invented in 1888 in Washington D.C. The inventor was drinking a mint julep.

15. Sunscreen lotion was invented in Miami, Florida.

16. More than half of the patents registered since 1790 are owned by the United States.

17. Clark University in Massachusetts was where the birth control pill was invented.

18. The sewing machine was invented in Boston by Elias Howe in 1845.

19. The bundt pan was invented in Minnesota.

20. The stapler was invented in Spring Valley, Minnesota.

21. The first moving sidewalks debuted at the 1893 Columbian Exposition in Chicago.

22. The first rocket that successfully sent humans to the moon was built in Alabama.

23. Rigby, Idaho is known as "the birthplace of television."

24. In 1893, the first aquarium opened in Chicago.

25. In 1939, the first air-conditioned car was manufactured in Detroit, Michigan.

26. Alexander Graham Bell invented the metal detector in order to find a bullet in U.S. President James Garfield's chest.

27. The world's first telephone book had only 50 names. It was published in New Haven, Connecticut in 1878.

28. The inventor of the strobe light was from Nebraska.

29. The first slot machine was invented by Charles Fey in 1899 in Nevada.

30. Hard hats for construction workers were invented in 1933 for people working on the Hoover Dam.

31. The alarm clock was invented in 1787 in New Hampshire.

32. The first submarine ride happened in the Passaic river in New Jersey. It was piloted by John P. Holland, the inventor of the submarine.

33. The world's first atomic bomb was detonated in 1945 in New Mexico at a testing range.

34. Toilet paper was invented in 1857 in New York City.

35. An Ohio man invented the cash register in 1879 because his customers kept stealing profits.

36. The first computer lived in Philadelphia in 1946.

Demographics

1. 40% of the women who give birth in the United States are not married.

2. About 25% of all prisoners in the world are in the United States.

3. About 33% of American children today grow up in homes with only one parent.

4. 37% of single mothers in the U.S. are living in poverty, while only 7% of married mothers in the U.S. are living in poverty.

5. In 2013, more women than men earned college degrees in the United States.

6. More men than women in America believe that having children is a measure of success.

7. According to one study, 42% of Americans believe in ghosts.

8. Indiana means "Land of the Indians." However, there are less than 8,000 Native Americans in the state of Indiana today.

9. There are 25 million adults in America living with their parents.

10. 10% of Americans rent storage units outside of their homes.

11. There were 3 "races" on the first U.S. census: Free White Females and Males, Slaves, and All Other Free Persons.

12. 1 in 19 residents of Washington, D.C. is a lawyer.

13. 1 in 8 Americans lives in California.

14. The state of Hawai'i has no racial or ethnic majorities. Every racial and ethnic group represented is a minority.

15. High school dropouts in the United States are 8 times more likely than people who graduate to go to prison.

16. In 1930, the average woman in the U.S. owned 9 outfits. Today, the average woman in the U.S. owns 30 outfits.

17. The size of the average American house has tripled over the last 50 years.

18. The average American home contains more than 300,000 items.

19. In Washington, D.C., there are more telephones than people.

20. The Latino population in the United States owns more guns than the U.S. police force.

21. In the 1700s, Acadians were driven out of Canada because they wouldn't pledge their loyalty to the King of England. Their descendants are Cajuns, many of whom live in Louisiana.

22. The town of Jean Lafitte, Louisiana used to be a hideout for pirates.

23. The average American spends about 17 days per year watching commercials.

24. The United States' oldest culture is that of the Pueblo people in the southwest.

25. Native Americans have been living in New Mexico for around twenty thousand years.

26. The Vietnamese last name "Nguyen" is more common in the U.S. than it is in Vietnam.

27. Hawai'i is the most isolated populated land in the entire world. It is thousands of miles away from other population centers.

28. Half of the population of the United States lives within 500 miles of Columbus, Ohio.

29. In New York City, there are four times as many abandoned homes as there are homeless people.

30. There are more people of Scottish descent in the United States than there are in Scotland.

31. There are at least 84 Americans named "Lol."

32. One third of the population of North Dakota is of Norwegian descent.

33. Between 1990 and 2000, approximately 10 million more people entered the U.S. than left it.

History – Part Two

1. Philadelphia was originally the capital of the U.S. Washington DC didn't become the capital until 1790.

2. George Washington Carver, who was born in the state of Alabama, discovered over 300 uses for peanuts.

3. Helium was discovered at the University of Kansas in 1905.

4. In 1894, Coca-Cola was bottled for the first time in the state of Mississippi.

5. Before the state of Tennessee became "Tennessee," it was known as "Franklin."

6. In March 1933, all U.S. banks were closed for one week to keep people from taking all of their money out.

7. In 1904 at the St. Louis World's Fair, iced tea was served for the first time.

8. In 1878, over 25% of the population of Memphis, Tennessee died of yellow fever.

9. The first rockets to be deployed in the United States were set off in 1812 by the British.

10. The Declaration of Independence was signed by one shoemaker: Roger Sherman.

11. In 1847, the U.S. captured Mexico City.

12. There have been 27 versions of the official flag of the United States.

13. Same-sex marriage became legal throughout the United States in 2015. In the years immediately before the Supreme Court ruling, same-sex marriage was only legal in some states.

14. In 1820, a 5-acre "national greenhouse" was built to grow plants to send around the country.

15. In the 1840s, there was a movement in the United States to create a new German state within Texas. Around 7,000 Germans immigrated to Texas during that time.

16. About 710,000 immigrants arrived in the United States in the first fifty years after the country was established.

17. Abraham Lincoln, President of the Union, and Jefferson Davis, President of the Confederacy, were born one year apart and less than a hundred miles away from one another. They were both born in Kentucky.

18. In the War of 1812, over half of the Americans killed were from Kentucky.

19. The first people who lived in the state of Maine were descendants of Ice Age hunters.

20. There is only one principality in the U.S. that has been under foreign rule. Eastport, Maine was ruled by Britain between 1814 and 1818.

21. In the 1500s, Native Americans were brought to England as slaves. Today, because of that, there are British people who are descendants of Native Americans.

22. New York was once a Dutch colony called New Amsterdam.

23. During the Civil War, more deaths were caused by disease than by combat.

24. The first rodeo in the world happened in Colorado on the Fourth of July in 1869.

25. The first emergency call to 911 in the United States was made in 1968 in Alabama. It was a Friday.

Landmarks and Monuments

1. The Statue of Liberty in New York wears a crown with seven rays. The rays, which each weigh up to 150 pounds, represent the seven continents.

2. The Liberty Bell, a famous national monument, was cracked in 1846 a few hours after it was last rung.

3. Los Angeles, California is home to the world's first motion-picture theater. It opened in 1902.

4. The world's oldest living tree, named "General Sherman," is located in California. It is 3,500 years old.

5. Hawai'i is home to the only royal palace in the United States.

6. The state of Minnesota is home to the oldest rock in the world. It is 3.8 billion years old.

7. The smallest park in the world can be found in Portland, Oregon. It measures 452 inches in total.

8. The only full-length statue of George Washington is located in the state of Virginia.

9. The state of Arizona is home to the largest meteorite crater in the world.

10. "Pennsylvania" is misspelled on the Liberty Bell. It's missing an N.

11. The U.S. Botanic Garden in Washington, D.C. is the oldest botanic garden in the United States that has been in use continually.

12. 800 million pounds of stone were removed to create the Mount Rushmore monument.

13. Each of the World Trade Center buildings had their own zip code.

14. The largest mall in the U.S. is called the Mall of America.

15. In 1925, a 300-foot-tall sequoia tree in California was named the national Christmas tree.

16. The oldest tourist attraction in the U.S. is Niagara Falls in New York.

17. The second oldest tourist attraction in the U.S. is Mammoth Cave in Kentucky. It was first promoted in 1816.

18. There are 2 mobile national monuments in the U.S.: The Saint Charles streetcar line in New Orleans and the cable cars in San Francisco.

19. Niagara Falls stopped flowing for 30 hours in 1848 because of ice blocking its flow.

20. The Empire State Building contains over 10 million bricks.

21. The Willis Tower, the John Hancock Center, One World Trade Center, and the Burj Khalifa were all designed by the same architectural company.

22. The Statue of Liberty was originally intended to be placed in Egypt's Suez Canal.

23. Texas has a masonry column that's 13 feet taller than the Washington Monument. It commemorates Texas's independence from Mexico and is the tallest masonry column in the world.

24. There is a statue of the world's largest bullhead fish in Crystal Lake, Iowa.

25. Rockport, Massachusetts is home to a house made entirely of newspaper.

26. About 102 people visit the Dr. Pepper museum in Texas each day.

27. Hoover Dam, located in Nevada, was the largest single public works project in U.S. history.

28. White Sands National Monument is a desert in New Mexico, but it's not made of sand.

29. The Mall of America is owned by Canadians.

30. In 1945, a U.S. Army airplane crashed into the 79th floor of the Empire State Building in New York.

31. In North Dakota, there is a 50-foot-tall pyramid of empty oil cans. It may be the tallest oil can tower in the world.

32. Nashville, Tennessee is home to the only reproduction of the Greek Parthenon.

33. On the façade of the National Cathedral in Washington, D.C., there is a carving of Star Wars' Darth Vader.

34. In Virginia, there is a foam replica of Stonehenge called Foamhenge.

35. The carved heads at Mount Rushmore sit in front of a hidden vault. The vault, which is not accessible to the public, contains the texts of the Declaration of Independence, the Constitution, and the Bill of Rights.

36. The second most visited house in the U.S. is Elvis Presley's Memphis, Tennessee home. It's known as Graceland.

States – Part Two

1. The city of Battle Creek, Michigan produces more breakfast cereal than any other city in the world.

2. The state of Louisiana has 2,482 small islands.

3. Colorado's Highway 550 was paved with low-grade gold. It is known as the Million Dollar Highway.

4. Although it's listed as the 17th state, the state of Ohio wasn't officially part of the United States until 1953.

5. California is home to about 500,000 earthquakes each year.

6. The most winding street in the world is in Burlington, Iowa. It is known as "Snake Alley."

7. Venus fly trap plants are native to South Carolina and North Carolina. They are not native to any other place in the world.

8. The world's highest roller coaster is in the state of New Jersey.

9. In Salt Lake City, Utah, it is illegal to carry an unwrapped ukulele in public.

10. 98% of the country's blueberries are grown in the state of Maine.

11. The world's busiest airport is in Atlanta, Georgia.

12. The oldest working airport in the United States is in Maryland.

13. The state of Minnesota is known as "the land of 10,000 lakes." However, the state of Wisconsin has more lakes than Minnesota.

14. The state of Pennsylvania contains the longest stone arch bridge in the world.

15. The world's largest amphitheater is in Hollywood, California.

16. The longest cave system in the world extends for over 200 miles. It's found in the U.S. state of Kentucky.

17. The only U.S. state that has an embassy in Washington, D.C. is Florida.

18. The second largest citrus fruit producer in the world is the state of Florida.

19. New Jersey is known as the diner capital of the world. There are about 525 diners in the state.

20. The state of Virginia is home to the world's only oyster museum.

21. The state of California has about the same population size as the country of Poland.

22. The population of Virginia is about the same size as the population of Switzerland.

23. The state of Illinois has a larger population than all of Portugal.

24. Pennsylvania's population is larger than the population of Greece.

25. Ohio's population is bigger than Belgium's.

26. The state of Maine has no poisonous snakes.

27. Streets in a Nevada town were once paved with silver. When locals discovered this, they ripped up the streets in 2 days.

28. The state Capitol of Texas is 15 feet taller than the Capitol of the United States.

29. The state of Kentucky has a Pledge of Allegiance to its state flag.

30. The state of Kentucky has an official state silverware pattern.

31. The state of Georgia became a state on a Wednesday in 1788.

Food and Drink – Part Three

1. Le Mars, Iowa is called the "Ice Cream Capital of the World" because it produces so much ice cream.

2. The state of Kansas produces enough wheat every year to feed the world's population for 2 weeks.

3. The first ice cream cones were created by accident at the 1904 St. Louis World's Fair. An ice cream vendor ran out of cups and asked a waffle vendor for help.

4. The potato chip was invented in 1853 when a New York chef sliced potatoes very thinly in response to a customer's complaint.

5. Pepsi was invented in 1867 in North Carolina. It was originally advertised as a health drink.

6. The first commercially grown tomato was grown in 1870 in Ohio.

7. In 2007, the watermelon became the state vegetable of Oklahoma. Watermelons are considered fruit in most other places.

8. A third of all tortillas produced in the United States are made in Texas.

9. Every apple in the state of Washington is picked by hand.

10. The state of Wisconsin produces over 600 different kinds of cheese.

11. There are over 152,000 fast food restaurants in the United States.

12. In the U.S., about one McDonald's Big Mac is sold every 17 seconds.

13. Americans spend an average of $100 per person on fast food every month.

14. The United States fast food industry generates about $208 billion each year.

15. The average American fast food meal has about 836 calories.

16. 24% of Americans think that fast food is healthy.

17. 3% of Americans eat a fast food meal every day. 4% of Americans never eat fast food.

18. Each year, the average U.S. supermarket throws away around 3,000 pounds of food.

19. Around 20% of the garbage in U.S. landfills is edible food.

20. Alma, Arkansas is known as the Spinach Capital of the World.

21. Fallbrook, California is the Avocado Capital of the World.

22. California grows over 300,000 tons of grapes every year.

23. Fresno, California calls itself the Raisin Capital of the World.

24. Castroville, California is known as the Artichoke Capital of the World.

25. The Pinto Bean Capital of the World is Dove Creek, Colorado.

26. The biggest producer of peaches, peanuts, and pecans in the U.S. is the state of Georgia.

27. The Vidalia onion, the sweetest onion in the world, can only be grown near Vidalia, Georgia.

28. Over 33% of pineapples sold around the world comes from Hawai'i.

Presidents – Part Two

1. There are 4 National Park sites named after Abraham Lincoln. There are another 4 named after Teddy Roosevelt.

2. The swivel chair was invented by Thomas Jefferson.

3. President Andrew Jackson taught his parrot how to say curse words.

4. There was a pet goat living at the White House when William Henry Harrison was president.

5. Only one U.S. president never got married: James Buchanan.

6. Abraham Lincoln was a wrestler.

7. President Warren G. Harding lost the White House china collection in a poker game.

8. In 1973, Jimmy Carter claimed that he saw a UFO.

9. George W. Bush was once a head cheerleader.

10. 30 United States presidents served in the U.S. Army.

11. 24 U.S. Presidents served in the U.S. Army during a time of war.

12. George Washington gave the shortest inaugural address in American history. It was 135 words long.

13. William Henry Harrison delivered his inaugural address in the snow. He was not wearing a hat or a coat. He died of pneumonia a few weeks later.

14. Four U.S. presidents were born in Norfolk County, Massachusetts. Three of them were named John.

15. In William Taft's presidential election campaign, inspired by the popularity of President Roosevelt's "Teddy Bear," Taft supporters tried to popularize a stuffed possum.

16. U.S. President Zachary Taylor voted in a presidential election for the very first time at age 62. He voted for himself.

17. Dick Cheney's dog was banned from Camp David because it attacked President Bush's dog.

18. Presidents Harrison, Polk, and Taylor all had severe stomach problems when they lived in the White House. It was probably due to contaminated water running through the building.

19. The richest president in the history of the United States was George Washington.

20. Teddy Roosevelt volunteered to serve in the U.S. military during World War I. He had already been president of the United States ten years earlier.

21. President Teddy Roosevelt killed a cougar with a knife.

22. All except for 5 presidents of the United States have worked either as lawyers or in the military.

23. Teddy Roosevelt was the first American to achieve a brown belt in Judo.

24. During George Washington's election campaign for the Virginia House of Burgesses, he gave 164 gallons of alcohol to 396 voters to win their favor. He won the election.

25. Abraham Lincoln once spent 24 hours unconscious after a horse kicked him in the head.

26. John Adams had a pet dog. Its name was Satan.

27. James Madison had two Vice Presidents. They both died in office.

28. By the time George Washington died, he only had one tooth left that was his own.

29. Barack Obama collected Spiderman and Conan the Barbarian comic books.

30. George Washington had false teeth made out of whale bone.

Music

1. The tune of the national anthem of the United States was taken from an English drinking song.

2. In 1977, New York City faced a massive electricity blackout during which a significant amount of DJ equipment was stolen from electronics stores. Soon after the blackout, the relatively unknown genre of hip hop gained widespread popularity.

3. The musical genre of jazz is thought to be the first genre of music to come out of the United States.

4. The first CD that was made for commercial purposes in the United States was Bruce Springsteen's Born in the USA.

5. Elvis Presley was once called "a savage" by a Florida judge who believed that Elvis's music was "undermining the youth."

6. Stephen Foster, who is known as the Father of American Music, wrote over 200 popular songs in the 1800s. He was born on July 4, 1826, America's Independence Day.

7. Over the last 80 years, several U.S. companies have claimed the rights to the "Happy Birthday" song. It is estimated that commercial uses of the song bring Warner Music around $2 million each year in royalties.

8. The music video for Michael Jackson's "Billie Jean" was the first music video by a black musician that appeared on MTV.

9. There is an annual David Bowie vs. Prince themed bicycle ride in Portland, Oregon.

10. In 1976, musician Barry Manilow's "I write the songs" topped music charts. He didn't write the song.

11. New Orleans is considered the birthplace of Jazz music. It emerged around 1895.

12. The song "Yankee Doodle," which became one of the most patriotic songs in the U.S., was origi-

nally written by a British surgeon making fun of colonial New Englanders.

13. The first streaming music system began in New York in 1897. People could connect to the Telharmonium through their telephones and listen to two musicians playing for 24 hours a day.

14. In the 1980s, Tipper Gore tried to sensor rock music in the U.S.

15. In Nairobi, Kenya, there is a thriving American country music scene.

16. NASA has its own radio station. It plays rock, indie, and alternative music.

17. The state of Florida passed a law that requires toddlers in state-run schools to listen to classical music every day.

Random Facts – Part Two

1. Minneapolis, Minnesota has a 52-block skyway system downtown. It's possible to eat, work, shop, and live within the system without going outside.

2. Hell's Half Acre is a popular nickname given to a diverse array of places around the United States. A "Hell's Half Acre" might have gotten its name due to a harsh landscape, a heavy drinking culture, a historical battle, a poverty problem, or a large minority population.

3. Kansas has an underground salt museum that houses government documents.

4. The first U.S. flag planted on the moon was blown away during the space craft's departure.

5. Fort Atkinson, Nebraska is home to the world's only fur trading museum.

6. The world's biggest gold producer is South Africa. The second largest is the state of Nevada.

7. The "Loneliest Highway in America" is located in Nevada. It has very few road stops over its 287-mile stretch between Ely and Fernley.

8. Inside the Cal-Neva building at Lake Tahoe, you can stand in both Nevada and California. Frank Sinatra once owned the building.

9. The longest morse code telegram ever sent contained the Nevada state constitution. It was sent from Nevada to Washington, D.C. in 1864.

10. The state of New Hampshire was named by Captain John Smith in honor of the town of Hampshire in England.

11. The state seal of New Jersey was designed in 1777 by a man who was born in Switzerland.

12. About 75% of roads in New Mexico are unpaved because the climate is so dry. They aren't in danger of being washed away.

13. Albuquerque, New Mexico was originally founded as a Spanish farming community.

14. On May 3, 1999, Oklahoma was hit by a tornado that had history's fastest recorded tornado wind speeds. It caused over a billion dollars in damage.

15. The New York Post is the oldest running newspaper in the U.S. It was established in 1803 by Alexander Hamilton.

16. Rochester, New York is both the Flour City and the Flower City.

17. The word "Croatoan" carved into a tree is the only remaining trace of America's first English colony at Roanoke Island.

18. There is a bridge in Ohio that is thought to be the only bridge in the world that you can cross and remain on the same side of the river.

19. Akron, Ohio is known as the rubber capital of the world.

20. Sumter, South Carolina is home to the world's largest ginkgo tree farm.

21. During the Manhattan Project, babies born in Los Alamos, New Mexico received birth certificates listing "P.O. Box 1663" as their place of birth.

22. New York City has a 550-foot-tall skyscraper with no windows. It was built that way so that it could withstand a nuclear blast.

23. 80% of drowning victims in the U.S. are male.

24. 90% of U.S.-made disco balls are manufactured in Kentucky.

25. The place farthest from any ocean in North America is also the poorest place in the U.S. That place is Allen, South Dakota.

26. El Paso, Texas is closer to California than it is to Dallas, Texas.

27. The city that's located in the center of Utah is named "Levan," or "navel" spelled backwards.

28. The Toilet Paper Capital of the World is Green Bay, Wisconsin.

29. In 1880, the age of consent in the state of Delaware was 7.

30. Almost everyone who lives in the town of Whittier, Alaska lives in the same building. The building contains a school, a hospital, a police department, a church, a grocer, and the mayor's office.

31. After the American Revolution, the Prince of Prussia was asked to become King of the United States. The offer was quickly rescinded.

International Relations

1. Between 2011 and 2013, China used more cement than the United States did in the entire 20th century.

2. In 2014, Canadian police killed 14 people, Chinese police killed 12 people, and German police killed no one. The same year, American police killed 1,100 people.

3. To get to the U.S. city of Point Roberts, Washington, you have to go through Canada.

4. The King of Thailand was born in Massachusetts, which means he's technically an American citizen.

5. One U.S. child has as much of an environmental impact as 280 children in Haiti.

6. Warren G. Harding, the first U.S. president to visit Canada, visited because he was on his way to Alaska.

7. The Pentagon building was built during World War II, when Italy was an enemy of the United States. Because marble came from Italy, there is no marble in the building.

8. 1% of the national budget of the United States is designated as aid for other countries.

9. Chicago, Illinois is colder than Iceland in the winter.

10. 80% of the active ingredients in U.S. drugs come from other countries.

11. The country of Liberia was founded by former Mississippi slaves who were freed in 1834.

12. Between 1969 and 1997, North Korea bought over 100 full-page ads in The New York Times, The Washington Post, and The Guardian to promote its political philosophy.

13. The official currency of Turks and Caicos is the U.S. dollar. It is a British territory.

14. The U.S. government used balloons to take photographs to spy on the Soviet Union. The Soviet Union used film recovered from these balloons to take pictures of the far side of the moon.

15. There is one North American gem included in England's Crown Jewels: The Montana Yogo Sapphire.

16. In 1905, the Russo-Japanese War ended with a treaty in the state of New Hampshire. The state is the only one that has hosted the formal conclusion of a foreign war.

17. Present day New Mexico, most of Colorado and Arizona, and parts of Texas, Utah, Kansas, Oklahoma, and Wyoming were once part of Spanish New Mexico.

18. In 1967, Russia and the United States signed a treaty agreeing not to launch nuclear weapons at the Moon.

19. The border between Oregon and California was established in 1819 by a treaty between the U.S. and Spain.

20. North America's first log cabins were built in 1683 by Swedish immigrants in Delaware.

21. In 1784, part of Alaska was settled by Russian fur traders and whalers.

22. In 1741, a Danish explorer discovered Alaska during a trip from Siberia.

23. In 1867, the U.S. offered to pay Russia two cents per acre to purchase Alaska.

24. The U.S. Senate never ratified the Treaty of Versailles. Because of this, it is legal to produce champagne in California.

25. In 1995, Russian President Boris Yeltsin was found on a street in Washington D.C., drunk, in his underwear, and trying to find pizza.

26. At their closest points, the U.S. and Russia are only 3.8 km apart.

27. Half of all nail salons in the U.S. are owned by Vietnamese immigrants.

28. Millions of chopsticks used in China are made in the United States.

29. In 1945, a 400-year-old bonsai tree survived the nuclear blast at Hiroshima, Japan. It was later given to the U.S. as a gift from Japan.

30. The Conflict Kitchen, a Pittsburgh restaurant, only serves food from countries with which the U.S. is currently in conflict.

31. There are residential houses located on the border between the U.S. and Canada that are partly in the U.S. and partly in Canada.

32. Maine was once captured by the British and named a Canadian province. It was called New Ireland. It was returned to the U.S. in a peace treaty.

Entertainment

1. The average American uses an electronic device for more than 10 hours per day.

2. The state of Nebraska is home to the world's only roller skating museum.

3. The Diving Capital of the World is Key Largo, Florida.

4. There is only one wooden carousel in the U.S. that still has its original paint. It is located in Burlington, Colorado and was built in 1905.

5. The oldest still-publishing newspaper in the U.S. was established in 1764.

6. Superman's home, Metropolis, is a real place in southern Illinois.

7. Topeka, Kansas was renamed "ToPikachu" for one day in 1998 when Pokemon arrived in the U.S.

8. The first public park in the U.S. was Boston Common. It became a park in 1634.

9. 70% of the silent films produced in the United States have been totally lost.

10. Massachusetts is home to a museum of horrible artwork.

11. There is a 16,000-square-foot ice rink in Reno, Nevada that was once dismantled and moved from Atlantic City, New Jersey.

12. The Flamingo, a famous Las Vegas casino, was named after a showgirl with long legs.

13. In 1999, there was one slot machine for every 10 residents in Nevada.

14. The first casino to open on what would eventually become the Las Vegas Strip was the Pair-O-Dice Club. It opened on Highway 91 in 1931.

15. In 1963, the U.S.'s first legal lottery began in New Hampshire.

16. The street names in the game Monopoly come from Atlantic City in New Jersey.

17. The world's largest international hot air balloon fiesta occurs in Albuquerque, New Mexico every October.

18. There is a town in New Mexico called The City of Truth or Consequences. It was named after the title of a radio quiz show.

19. The first circus in the U.S. opened in 1774 in Newport, Rhode Island.

20. In 1964, New York City hosted the first ever comic convention. Among its 30 participants was a teenager named George R.R. Martin.

21. Pennsylvania once had a strip club with a drive-thru. Customers could pay $10 per minute to watch the indoor activity from their cars.

22. Miss USA 1957 was stripped of her title when it was discovered that she was married and had two children.

23. The first movie in the U.S. to show a toilet flushing was Psycho, released in 1960. It was very controversial.

24. There are more clowns per capita in North Dakota than in any other state.

25. The game of Pictionary was invented in the state of Washington.

26. During World War II, about 90% of Disney employees in the U.S. helped make propaganda and training videos.

27. The Detroit Zoo was established when a circus went bankrupt while in the city.

Notable Americans

1. American Civil Rights activist Martin Luther King, Jr. was given the name "Michael" when he was born. His name was changed to "Martin" when he was 5 years old.

2. Joseph Spinney was mayor of Fresno, California for only ten minutes.

3. Marilyn Monroe was named the first Artichoke Queen of Castroville, California in 1947.

4. In 1809, Mary Kies became the first woman to receive a U.S. patent for weaving straw with silk.

5. Noah Webster, the author of the 1807 dictionary, was born in West Hartford, Connecticut.

6. Joe Bowen once walked 3,008 miles on stilts from Bowen, Kentucky to Los Angeles, California.

7. One U.S. Supreme Court Chief Justice was born in jail: Frederick Vinson.

8. A bra that was worn by Marilyn Monroe sold for $14,000.

9. The first governor of Arkansas was painted in a portrait by Samuel Morse, the man who invented morse code.

10. The first performer to stage-dive was Iggy Pop. He did so at a concert in Detroit, Michigan.

11. In 1930, baseball player Babe Ruth had a higher salary than the president of the United States.

12. Elvis Presley was a distant relative of U.S. Presidents Jimmy Carter and Abraham Lincoln.

13. The voice of Mickey Mouse married the voice of Minnie Mouse in 1991.

14. There is a steakhouse in Manhattan that houses tobacco pipes that once belonged to Albert Einstein, Babe Ruth, and Teddy Roosevelt.

15. Martha Stewart was featured in Glamour magazine in 1961 as one of ten "Best-Dressed College Girls."

16. An American flag has been over the site of Francis Scott Key's birthplace continuously since

1949. Francis Scott Key is the author of the national anthem of the United States.

17. President Andrew Johnson demeaned a deaf person in the 1860s. The man eventually became the first deaf lawyer in the United States.

18. There is an annual Munchkins parade in the New York hometown of L. Frank Baum, the author of The Wizard of Oz.

19. The oldest man to go into outer space was John Glenn, a senator from Ohio. He traveled into space in 1998, when he was 77 years old.

20. Roger Williams, the founder of Rhode Island, was banished from Plymouth, Massachusetts for supporting freedom of speech and freedom of religion.

21. Morgan Freeman owns a 124-acre beekeeping farm in Mississippi.

22. Walt Disney once worked at a local newspaper in Missouri. He was fired because he wasn't creative enough.

23. The first English baby born in America was named Virginia Dare. She was born in the Roa-

noke Colony in present-day North Carolina in 1587.

Big America – Part Two

1. The world's largest man-made geyser in the world is Soda Springs, located in the state of Idaho.

2. The world's largest public library has over 2 million books. It's located in Chicago, Illinois.

3. Chicago, Illinois is home to the world's largest cookie and cracker factory. It's owned by Nabisco and produced 16 billion Oreo cookies in 1995.

4. The world's largest strawberry was grown in Iowa.

5. There is a ball of twine in Kansas that weighs over 16,750 pounds.

6. The world's biggest free-swinging bell is located in Newport, Kentucky. It's known as the World Peace Bell.

7. Pike County, Kentucky is the largest producer of coal in the world.

8. The world's largest cast iron statue is located in Birmingham, Alabama. "The Vulcan" weighs 120,000 pounds.

9. Boston's Children's Museum has a giant milk bottle that could hold 50,000 gallons of milk.

10. The world's largest cement plant is located in Alpena, Michigan.

11. The Mall of America is as big as 78 football fields.

12. The state of California has a larger population than the country of Canada.

13. The Old Spanish Fort Museum in Pascagoula, Mississippi displays the world's largest shrimp.

14. Edwards, Mississippi is home to the largest cactus plantation in the world.

15. In 2015, the U.S. Postal Service ordered over 888 million rubber bands.

16. The world's largest rodeo occurs each year in Denver, Colorado.

17. The tallest man documented in medical history was from St. Louis, Missouri. He was 8 feet, 11.1 inches tall.

18. About 20% of the world's garbage is produced in the United States.

States – Part Three

1. The U.S. city with the most golfers per capita is Minneapolis, Minnesota.

2. The Cotton Capital of the World, the Catfish Capital of the World, the Sweet Potato Capital of the World, and the Towboat Capital of the World are all located in the state of Mississippi.

3. The University of Texas was established by the constitution of the state of Texas.

4. There is only one state that shares a border with just one other state: Maine.

5. Kentucky is known as the Bluegrass State. Bluegrass is actually green.

6. In West Virginia, it's perfectly legal to take home road kill and eat it for dinner.

7. The state of Kansas is home to 27 Walnut Creeks.

8. Montana has at least 5 ghost towns. One is named Pony.

9. Nebraska used to be known as the "Tree Planter's State." In 1945, its nickname changed to the "Cornhusker State."

10. There is only one U.S. state that has a single-house legislature. That state is Nebraska.

11. Every county in New Jersey is classified as a metropolitan area. It's the only state in the U.S. that classifies every county as such.

12. New Jersey is home to more toxic waste dumps than any other state in the U.S.

13. The town of Delmar is located in two states: Maryland and Delaware.

14. In 1947 and in 1989, lawmakers in North Dakota tried to rename the state "Dakota." The state legislature rejected both attempts.

15. Oregon's state flag has a separate design on its reverse side. It pictures a beaver.

16. There are only two states with no self-serve gas stations: Oregon and New Jersey.

17. At the point where Northern California meets Southern California, there is a pine tree and a palm tree planted next to each other. The trees symbolize the start of the southern and northern parts of the state.

18. New Mexico Magazine has a regular column documenting incidents of U.S. businesses mistaking New Mexico for a foreign country.

19. In 1777, the year Vermont abolished slavery, the state was an independent republic. Technically, it was the first country in the Americas to abolish slavery.

20. Queen Elizabeth is an admiral of the state of Nebraska. The honor gives her control of the state's officers, seamen, tadpoles, and goldfish.

21. When the state of Georgia was founded, it had three prohibitions: no slavery, no alcohol, and no Catholics.

22. There is a Missouri county shaped like Utah. Its name is Texas.

23. In 1784, part of North Carolina seceded and called itself Franklin. It would have become the 14th state, but it needed 2 more votes.

24. Alaska has no counties. This means that the northernmost county in the U.S. is in Minnesota.

25. No one knows whether North Dakota or South Dakota became a state first.

26. The Virginia state flag is the only state flag to include nudity.

27. In the Civil War, Tennessee was both the last state to secede from and the first state to be re-admitted into the Union.

28. Since 1519, the state of Texas has faced eight changes of government. It has been under the rule of Spain, France, Mexico, the Republic of Texas, the Confederate States, and the United States.

29. Between 1836 and 1845, Texas was an independent nation.

30. The state of Rhode Island is small enough to fit inside of certain ranches in Texas.

31. In Kentucky, there are more whiskey barrels than people.

Holidays

1. Musician Stevie Wonder was at the forefront of the campaign to make Martin Luther King Jr. Day a national holiday in the U.S.

2. Three towns in the U.S. are called "Santa Claus."

3. The holiday of Mardi Gras was introduced to the West in the state of Alabama.

4. The town of Santa Claus, Indiana receives over half a million letters to Santa Claus every Christmas.

5. The city of Loveland, Colorado re-mails hundreds of thousands of Valentine's Day letters each year.

6. In Chicago, residents dye the river green for every Saint Patrick's Day.

7. Mother's Day was created by a teacher in Kentucky in 1887.

8. There is a holiday in the U.S. that celebrates the country's flag. However, Flag Day is an official holiday in only one state: Pennsylvania.

9. Each year, Americans spend around $7 billion on Halloween.

10. There's about a 25% chance that it will snow in New York on Christmas.

11. About $310 million was spent on pet Halloween costumes in the U.S. in 2011.

12. Each March, the state of Illinois celebrates Casimir Pulaski Day to honor a Polish war hero. Pulaski never even visited the American Midwest.

13. In South Dakota, Columbus Day has been abolished. The day is celebrated instead as Native American Day.

14. Father's Day accounts for the highest tie and neck wear sales each year in the United States.

15. Each year on Mother's Day, restaurant sales and church attendance are notably high in the United States.

16. One sixth of all turkeys consumed each year in the United States are eaten on Thanksgiving.

More Books by Bill O'Neill

Please,

if you liked this book, leave a review on Amazon, it helps me a lot! Make sure you check out the rest of my books on Amazon.

Until next time,
Bill O'Neill

Made in the USA
San Bernardino, CA
18 May 2020